THE ORDER OF PLANETS IN VIMSHOTTARI DASHA

THE ORDER OF PLANETS IN VIMSHOTTARI DASHA

AWODELE

BEKH

UNION, KY ™

BEKH, LLC
UNION, KY
BEKHLLC@OUTLOOK.COM

ISBN-10: 0692380256
ISBN-13: 978-0692380253

DEDICATION

This book is dedicated to those seekers who dare to look beyond what is on the surface in order to penetrate and understand the depths of this great science.

TABLE OF CONTENTS

TABLE OF FIGURES

~

INTRODUCTION

It was during my undergraduate college years (1993 - 1997) when I purchased my first book on Vedic Astrology. The title of the book was *Ancient Hindu Astrology for the Modern Western Astrologer* by James T. Braha. Not having any software at the time, I was able to create my tropical chart with planetary positions using a free chart generator on the internet. Using the information in Braha's book, I learned how to deduct the ayanamsa value from the tropical positions of the planets to obtain their sidereal positions. In addition, Braha's book introduced me to Vimshottari Dasha and provided instructions on how to manually calculate the Dasha periods.

Vimshottari, which means 120, is a Nakshatra based Dasha unique to Vedic Astrology. It is composed of nine periods of varying lengths, each ruled by one of the nine planets of Vedic Astrology. In all, the length of these periods total 120 years for which it is named. The periods run in the following order listed below, but an individual can be born into any of the periods (beginning, middle, end) based on the longitude of the Moon at the time of birth. After the remainder of the initial period is completed, the next period follows in sequence.

Dasha Ruler/Period	Length in Years
Ketu	7
Venus	20
Sun	6
Moon	10
Mars	7
Rahu	18
Jupiter	16
Saturn	19
Mercury	17

After my initial exposure to Vimshottari through Braha's book, and attempting to understand how it applied to my chart, one of the questions that naturally came to mind concerned the allotment of years to each of the Dasha rulers. To me they seemed random & non-uniform, causing me to wonder as to the origin & basis of the allotment of years in this system. Another question that naturally came to mind concerned the basis for the order of planets in this system. Possessing a deep desire to find an answer, I set out to obtain as much information as I could on the subject. Unfortunately, one of the many things I discovered during my quest is that published material explaining the reason behind the allotment of years and order of planets is scarce.

One of the rare books that mentioned anything regarding the basis for the allotment of years and order of planets in Vimshottari was *Hindu Astrology Lessons: 36 Teachers Share Their Wisdom*. In this book, there is an article written by Narendra Desai who states on page 65 that as to the allocation of a certain number of years to each planet in Vimshottari Dasha to see the work of Dr. V.G. Rele (Vasant Gangaram Rele).

When I first read this passage I was beyond excitement. I was finally going to get an answer to one of these questions. With anxious enthusiasm, I went straight to the internet to do a search for Dr. Rele's book. Surprisingly, there was not much written about the contents of this book, but nonetheless, I was lucky enough to find a copy from a used book dealer and placed the online order. The title of the book is *Directional Astrology of the Hindus as Propounded in Vimshottari Dasha.*

As I began reading the book, I came across passages that resonated so well with my questions that I knew even before completing the book that it would become one of my favorites. On this, Dr. Rele writes on pages 6 & 7,

> *"It is a matter of great surprise that none of the books on the Jyotish Shastra explains upon what principle the various periods are allotted to several planets; even Parashara, to whom the origin of these Dasha is attributed, is silent upon the matter. . . When the system of Vimshottari Dasha was introduced into Astrological literature, by whom, and on what basis; why a particular order of planets is followed, why certain periods are assigned to certain planets, these are points which are surrounded with mystery and which require exposition."*

I assume that these comments were written in the early 1930's as the copy in my possession has a copyright date of 1935 and the preface is dated December 1934. Even now, almost eighty years after the publication of Dr. Rele's book, I can say that I have only been able to obtain material from a handful of authors who have attempted to provide answers to these mysteries.

With these things firmly fixated in my mind, I came across a subject in the Summer of 2009 that really grabbed my attention. I took the time that summer to learn more about it, but had to put it aside for awhile as I spent my time on other things. Upon further review of the subject in December of 2009, I was able to see a possible explanation for why the order of planets in Vimshottari Dasha follows the sequence that it does. So I decided in December 2009 to attempt to put in writing the connection I saw with Vimshottari and what is called Vortex-Based Mathematics. I had completed a manuscript in September 2011, but did not think I had enough material to publish a book. After coming across the manuscript and the work I had already done in late January 2015, I decided that it would be well worth it to proceed with publishing the material I had put together. It is my sincere hope that this will help to shed some light on unraveling the mystery behind the order of planets in Vimshottari Dasha.

Awodele

January 29, 2015

1

PAST THEORIES

Before providing a summary of the theories I have come across in my research, I think it is important for readers to understand that Vimshottari is just one of ten Nakshatra based Dashas, which are calculated based on the longitude of the Moon as it moves through the various Nakshatras or Lunar Mansions. Thus, in the opening chapter on the Dashas of the Planets in *Brihat Parasara Hora Sastra*, Parasara explains that Dashas are of many kinds and amongst them, Vimshottari is the most appropriate for the general population. He then goes on to list the other Dashas to be followed in special cases.

It must be noted that the conditional Dashas differ greatly from the structure of Vimshottari. In fact, they all differ from each other. For example, Vimshottari is the only one of these Dashas to have nine distinct periods, which are ruled by the nine planets. The remaining either have eight or seven periods where one or two of the nine planets are omitted. In addition, the number of years allotted to periods ruled by the same planet differ as well. In Vimshottari, the Moon rules its period for ten years while in Ashtottari it rules for fifteen years. Thus, when we talk about ascertaining the basis for the allocation of years to Vimshottari or its sequence, we must keep in mind that the other Dashas differ in the way they allocate years and how the Dasha Lords are sequenced. Maybe there is a relationship to how they are all structured and discovering the key for one can lead to insights in how the others are structured.

As I mentioned in the introduction, Vimshottari means 120. It is composed of nine periods of varying lengths, each ruled by one of the nine planets of Vedic Astrology. In all, the length of these periods total 120 years for which it is named. The periods run in the following sequence listed below.

Dasha Ruler/Period	Length in Years
Ketu	7
Venus	20
Sun	6
Moon	10
Mars	7
Rahu	18
Jupiter	16
Saturn	19
Mercury	17

I have only been able to obtain material from a handful of authors who have attempted to provide answers as to the allotment of years and order of periods listed above. I will now summarize each of their theories in the sections that follow.

Dr. Vasant G. Rele

Thankfully, Dr. Rele provides a valid explanation as to why the Dasha Lords were assigned the number of years they are said to rule in Vimshottari. In addition, he also provides a theory regarding the basis for the order of planets in this system.

As to the allotment of years to each of the planets, Dr. Rele first explains how the Zodiac of 360° is divided into three sections of 120° each. In each of these three sections, there are nine Nakshatra's, which are ruled by the nine Dasha Lord's in the following order: Ketu, Venus, Sun, Moon, Mars, Rahu, Jupiter, Saturn, and Mercury. Thus, the first Nakshatra of 13°20' is Aswini and is ruled by Ketu, the second, Bharani is ruled by Venus, etc. The last Nakshatra in the first section, Ashlesha, is ruled by Mercury to complete the first 120°.

Thus, with nine Nakshatras in each of the three 120° sections, there are twenty seven Nakshatras in total encompassing the full 360° Zodiac circle. Therefore, each of the planets rules three Nakshatras that are separated by 120° as shown in the diagram on the following page. There is much more in his book that I recommend the reader to take the time to read, but to summarize, Rele emphasizes that the trine is the basis of Vimshottari Dasha. On page 26 he goes on to say,

> "*If we take all the planets to be at the beginning in the Aswini Nakshatra, at the end of the period assigned to the planets they will be seen either in Magha or Mula Nakshatra, the only condition being that the planets must be visible in the sky in a Janma Nakshatra in trine to, or in conjunction with, its original Janma Nakshatra.*"

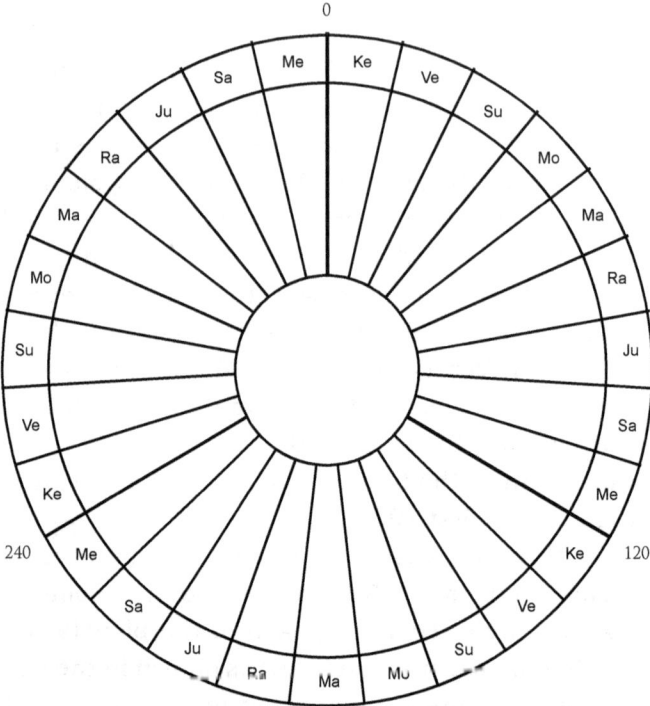

Figure 1: Trine as the Basis of Vimshottari

For example, if Saturn is visible in Aswini at the beginning of its period, it will come to Mula Nakshatra in Sagittarius, which is in trine to its original Aswini Nakshatra at the end of the nineteenth year. This matches the number of years assigned to Saturn in Vimshottari. Likewise, on page 31, Dr. Rele states that

> *"Jupiter having nearly the same motion as that of a Rashi Chakra a year, it can only come in trine, in or conjunction with, original Nakshatra at the end of the fourth, eighth, twelfth, and*

sixteenth years; but we find that at the end of the fourth year its actual geocentric place to form a trine is short by nearly 5 degrees. At the end of the eighth year it comes in Janma Mula Nakshatra, where it is mainly retrograde, and is ahead of the trine by nearly 5 degrees and too near the horizon to be visible. At the end of the twelfth year it is too near the sun in Aswini to be visible. It is only at the end of the sixteenth year that it comes nearly in trine to, or in conjunction with, the Yogatara of Magha Nakshatra and is perhaps visible just above the horizon."

The number of years assigned to Jupiter in Vimshottari is 16 years. In like fashion, the author provides explanations for the other planets in this system.

As to the order of planets in Vimshottari, Dr. Rele makes known that the arrangement of planets is neither geocentric nor heliocentric. Geocentric means earth-centered and can be interpreted as the order of planets as viewed from the earth. It can also be interpreted as the order of planets arranged in increasing orbital periods with respect to the body that planet orbits. The closest planet to the Earth is the Moon, which also orbits the Earth every 27.3 days. Mercury is next, with an orbital period around the Sun of 88 days. Likewise, the other planets follow in sequence with their orbital periods around the Sun as follows: Venus (225 days), Sun (365.25 days/1 year), Mars (1.88 years), Jupiter (12 years), and Saturn (30 years). Please keep in mind that it isn't the Sun's orbit around the Earth, but the Earth's orbit around the Sun that defines the year.

Heliocentric means sun-centered and is the order of planets going outward from the Sun in the solar system. The order is as follows: Sun, Mercury, Venus, Earth with the Moon, Mars, Jupiter, and Saturn. Notice that Rahu & Ketu are not represented in either model. Since the order of planets in Vimshottari does not match that of the Geocentric or Heliocentric models, Dr. Rele proceeds to ask the pertinent question, then why is the particular order followed in Vimshottari Moon, Mars, Rahu, Jupiter, Saturn, Mercury, Ketu, Venus, and Sun. He offers that maybe the originator of the system at one time observed this order in the sky and goes through a process to find if there was indeed a time when the planets would have been visible to the observer in the order of Vimshottari. The author provides a date when this arrangement actually occurred, but the reader is left wondering why this particular date & arrangement is so special as to set the order of planets in this system. Thus, it left me thinking that there was a better explanation still out there waiting to be found.

O. P. Verma

In relationship to Dr. Rele's book, O.P. Verma also offers an explanation as to the allocation of years to the planets in Vimshottari, and also provides rationale for the order of planets in a book entitled, *Secrets of Vimshottari Dasha*. Although Verma does not mention the work of Dr. Rele, the explanation provided as to the allocation of years assigned to each planet is the same as Dr. Rele's, although not as detailed. Curiously, the rationale that Verma offers for the order of planets is based on what he calls, their geocentric order. However, based on the geocentric order detailed above, the reader is left wondering if Verma's concept of geocentric order is quite different from the traditional. There is no mention of the nodes Rahu & Ketu in the traditional geocentric order, and the position of the Moon is out of place to correlate with Vimshottari. However, if you take the geocentric and heliocentric order of planets and compare them to each other, you will notice that the only difference between the two are the positions of the Sun and Moon.

Geo - <u>Moon</u>, Mercury, Venus, <u>Sun</u>, Mars, Jupiter, Saturn
Heli - <u>Sun</u>, Mercury, Venus, <u>Moon</u>, Mars, Jupiter, Saturn

If the nodes are inserted, and the Sun & Moon placed after Venus, it would indeed match the order of Vimshottari.

Dr. Kar

Another work related to this subject is an article written by Dr. Pt. K.R. Kar, Ph.D. (JB) entitled, *In Quest of Origin of Parasar's Vimshottary Dasa - Period*. I believe it was originally published in a magazine entitled *KP & Astrology*, but the scanned copy of the article I was able to obtain is from *K.P. Year Book - 2004*. I find it worth mentioning in the context of what has been discussed thus far because Dr. Kar provides his own unique theory as to the allocation of years to each of the planets in Vimshottari Dasha. However, I personally favor Dr. Rele's theory over that of Dr. Kar's.

Satyanarayana Naik

One of two remaining pieces of material that I am personally aware of that is related to the subject under discussion is a book entitled *K.P. Dynamics: Stellar Horary Astrology Redefined* by Satyanarayana Naik. In reference to Vimshottari Dasha, Naik states on page 2 of this book that

> ". . . none of the classical texts reveal the basis of allotment of number of years allotted to the planet."

Naik goes on to say on page 3 that he and his research team

> " . . . have started research in this field and have been success-
> ful in deriving at the astronomical phenomena to support many
> of the astrological dictums propounded by sage Parasara and
> Jaimini."

Being successful in such matters has led the research team to de-
rive the astronomical solution to the allotment of Dasha Periods to
the planets. Continuing on page 3, Naik states that his research
team

> " . . . will come out with their Magnum opus on this subject with
> astronomical details supporting the astrological theory."

At the time when I first put this manuscript together in 2011, I
was not aware of such a book being published, but was anxiously
waiting to hear what Naik and his research team had found. However, the past three to four years led me in other directions with my
research, and I had not followed up to see if Naik had his research
team had published this material. As I am in the process of updat-
ing this manuscript, I will be sure to check to see if this indeed has
been accomplished.

Drs. Frans Langenkamp

The last piece of material, and the most recent piece I have
is an article entitled, *The Basis of the Vimshottary Dasha System
found in Rig Veda* by Drs. Frans Langenkamp. Langenkamp states,

"The Rig Veda consists of ten Chapters called Mandalas. . . all the knowledge of the ten Mandalas of Rig Veda is concentratedly available in the first Mandala, consisting of 192 Suktas (hymns). Furthermore . . . all knowledge of the first Mandala is contained in concentrated form in the first Sukta, consisting of nine Richas (verses). Then it goes on to show that the knowledge of the first Sukta is contained in the first Richa, consisting of nine words."

In the article, Langenkamp describes what each of the first nine words of the Rig Veda means and shows how they are related to the nine planets in the order of Vimshottari. As Langenkamp suggests, the Rig Veda is said to be an encyclopedia of all the laws of nature, and thus, the arrangement and structure of its words, versus, hymns, and chapters are based on these laws. That said, the author of the Rig Veda must have been aware of a model that provided the basis for arranging and structuring its content in the manner intended. Seeing that there is a relationship between the structure of the Rig Veda and the order of Vimshottari, Langenkamp states that

"This suggests that the Vimshottary Dasha system has a very solid basis indeed! It is based on the primordial evolutionary sequence of Nature."

If Vimshottari Dasha is based on this same model, then what could it be?

With the above-mentioned things firmly fixated in my mind, I came across a subject in the Summer of 2009 that really grabbed my attention. I took the time that summer to learn more about it, but had to put it aside for awhile as I spent my time on other things. Upon further review of the subject in December of 2009, I was able to see a possible explanation for why the order of planets in Vimshottari Dasha follows the sequence that it does. After reading Langenkamp's article, which I found in the latter part of November 2010, I believe this subject to be the model that describes the primordial evolutionary sequence of Nature that he talks about.

Langenkamp also writes in his article concerning Vimshottari's connection to the Rig Veda that

> *"In the 25 years of my study of Vedic astrology, I never came across an explanation of why the planets in the Vimshottary Dasha system are arranged in that particular sequence. Not even an attempt to explain it ever appeared on the Jyotish horizon, as far as I know. I felt that the correspondence is rather striking, and it kept sticking in my mind. Therefore, I thought I should share it with all my colleague Jyotish students."*

This describes exactly how I feel and I thank Langenkamp for sharing the article with the public. I decided back in December 2009 to write a book showing the connection I saw with Vimshottari and the subject of the next chapter - Vortex-Based Mathematics. May this book help to shed some light on unraveling the mystery behind the order of planets in Vimshottari Dasha.

2

VORTEX-BASED MATHEMATICS

For those of you who are not familiar with the I Ching, it is an ancient Chinese book used for divination to seek guidance on how to conduct oneself in certain situations in order to be successful. It is composed of 64 hexagrams, which contain six lines each, and each of these six lines can be either Yin or Yang. Yang lines are depicted as solid, and Yin Lines are depicted as broken as shown below. In addition, hexagrams are constructed starting from the bottom and ending at the top.

Line Number	Hexagram
Line 6:	___ ___
Line 5:	_____
Line 4:	___ ___
Line 3:	_____
Line 2:	___ ___
Line 1:	_____

Since a binary number system represents numeric values using only two symbols, "0" and "1", each hexagram has the capacity to also function as a binary number. If we define the Yin line as a symbol that indicates "0", and the Yang line as a symbol that indicates "1", the hexagram depicted on the previous page is equivalent to binary number 101010 when reading it from bottom to top. This is depicted below.

Line Number	Hexagram	Binary	Symbol
Line 6:	___ ___	0	"Yin"
Line 5:	_____	1	"Yang"
Line 4:	___ ___	0	"Yin"
Line 3:	_____	1	"Yang"
Line 2:	___ ___	0	"Yin"
Line 1:	_____	1	"Yang"

To determine the numeric value that this binary number represents, you would take the number on each line and raise it to its corresponding power. This is depicted in the example below where "n" is representative of either "0" or "1".

Line Number	Formula
Line 6	n^{32}
Line 5	n^{16}
Line 4	n^{8}
Line 3	n^{4}
Line 2	n^{2}
Line 1	n^{1}

As you proceed from line one to line six, the powers double so that in line 2 there is a "2", and in line 3 there is a "4". This doubling will continue until you get to "32" in line 6. A binary system encompassing six columns or rows can represent a numeric value from "0" to "63". In the example given, binary number 101010 would convert to a numeric value via the calculations in the table below. Adding up the results of each line we get numeric value "21" (1 + 0 + 4 + 0 + 16 + 0). Therefore, binary number 101010 represents numeric value "21".

Line Number	Formula	Result
Line 6	0^{32}	= 0
Line 5	1^{16}	= 16
Line 4	0^8	= 0
Line 3	1^4	= 4
Line 2	0^2	= 0
Line 1	1^1	= 1

That said, in the early part of 2009 while studying the I Ching, I noticed that the powers "1, 2, 4, 8, 16, 32" repeat themselves if you continue the sequence beyond six lines. However, you have to reduce the numbers that are composed of more than 1 digit by a process of successive addition until you have a single digit. For example, "16" is equal to 1 + 6, which is "7". Likewise, "32" is equal to 3 + 2, which is "5". Hence, you get the number sequence "1, 2, 4, 8, 7, 5".

If you were to continue with the sequence beyond line six, it would repeat the pattern as "64" reduces to a "1" using successive addition (6 + 4 equals "10", and 1 + 0 equals "1"). Doubling "64", the next power would be "128" and 1 + 2 + 8 is "11", and 1 + 1 is "2".

Doubling "128" yields the next power "256", which is equivalent to the number 4 after successive addition. Upon realizing that there was a pattern, I immediately had a thought to do a search for the sequence "1, 2, 4, 8, 7, 5" on the internet. Sure enough, there was information written about the sequence. In particular, there was the research and work of an individual by the name of Marko Rodin. There were a series of Youtube videos (44 total) that I listened to over the course of the next couple days in which Rodin gave a lecture on what he calls Vortex-Based Mathematics. It is this math that serves as the basis for explaining the possible reason behind the order of planets in Vimshottari Dasha.

1	alif
2	ba
3	jim
4	dal
5	ha
6	waw
7	zay
8	ha
9	ta
10	ya
20	kaf
30	lam
40	mim
50	nun
60	sin
70	ayn
80	fa
90	sad
100	qaf
200	ra
300	shin
400	ta
500	tha
600	kha
700	dhal
800	dad
900	za

In the *Introduction and Summary of the Rodin Coil and Votex-Based Mathematics*, Marko discovered that in the Bahai faith, the Most Great name of the prophet Bahaullah is ABHA. He understood that names produce vibrations and wanted to obtain the precise mystical intonation of the name, so he converted each letter to a numeric value using the Abjad numerical notation system since the Bahai sacred scripture is originally written in Persian and Arabic. This was a sacred system of allocating a unique numerical value to each letter of the twenty seven letters of this alphabet, which is depicted to the right of this page.

As you can see, the "A" (alif) has a value of 1, "B" (ba) has a value of 2, and "H" (ha) has a value of 5. When these numbers are added together (1 + 2 + 5 + 1) the result is nine. Realizing that the name was equal to nine, and given the importance to this number throughout the Bahai scriptures, he then drew a circle and placed the number nine at the top with the rest of the numbers following in sequence proceeding clockwise around the circle. The result was an image similar to Figure 2-1 below.

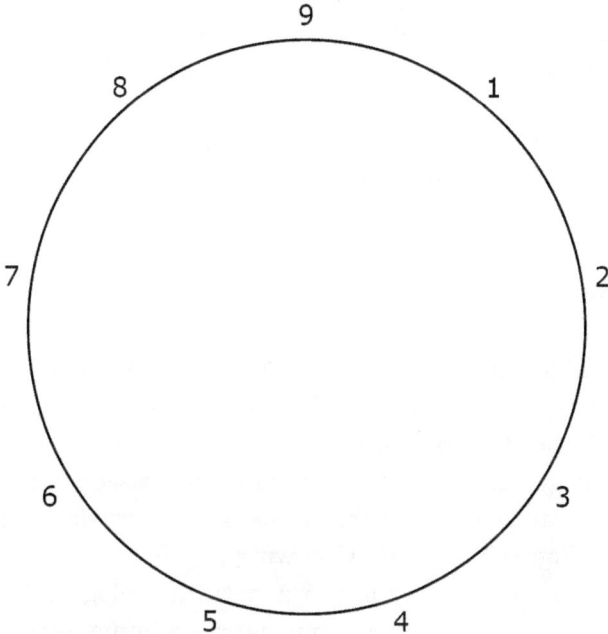

Figure 2-1: Circle of Nine

What Rodin discovered was a unique number system within this circle. As I did with the I Ching, numbers composed of more than one digit are reduced by successive addition of the digits within that number until there is only one digit remaining. Doing so, we find that there are only nine unique digits in the number system. For example, "10" is 1 + 0, which is equal to "1". Each number in sequence will reduce to a single digit creating the repeating pattern 1 through 9 as shown in the diagram above.

Even though Rodin started with the number nine positioned at the top, I would like to mention that before proceeding to the number one, the originating point at the top should be a zero. This has cosmological implications that I would like to tie in later. Please keep in mind that it naturally precedes the number one and therefore, occupies the same position as the number nine. Starting at zero and going clockwise through each number around the circle, we don't arrive at the number nine until we return to the point of origin. Therefore, the sequence of numbers can be said to form a cycle.

The Doubling/Halving Circuit

In addition to the circular sequence above, the pattern that I described earlier, "1, 2, 4, 8, 7, 5", can also be depicted within this diagram. Without lifting your pencil from the paper, you can draw this pattern by starting at "1" and continuing the sequence to "2", "4", "8", etc., until you get back to the point of origin at "1". This is depicted in Figure 2-2 on the following page.

The process of doubling is a natural biological function of cells called mitosis. Consider what happens immediately following conception in the human reproductive process. After the sperm and egg unite, this single cell begins a process by which it starts to divide. The single cell will divide into two identical cells. These two cells will each divide to bring the number to four. Once again, each of these four cells will divide, bringing the number to eight. This doubling process will continue, but the "1, 2, 4, 8, 7, 5" sequence will stay in sync. It also stays in sync when you half numbers with the exception that it follows the path in the reverse order. Starting with 1, we halve it to get .5, and then .5 becomes .25, and so on. When the respective digits making up each of these numbers are added together and further reduced to a single digit, the pattern is "1, 5, 7, 8, 4, 2".

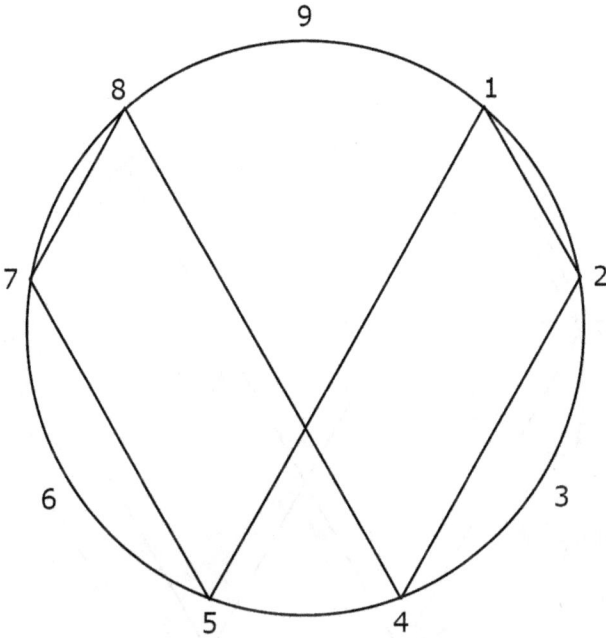

Figure 2-2: The Doubling/Halving Circuit

Oscillation

As you can see from the above diagram, the 3, 6, & 9 are not part of the doubling circuit because they create their own unique pattern. Starting with three, if you double it the result is six. If you double the six you get twelve, which equals a three (1 + 2). Twelve doubled is twenty-four, which equals six (2 +4). In this manner, the three and six always oscillates back and forth with nine as the control. Notice in Figure 3-3 below that three and six don't connect at the base because it is described as a vector. As Rodin explains in his youtube video, this creates the pattern "3, 9, 6, 6, 9, 3".

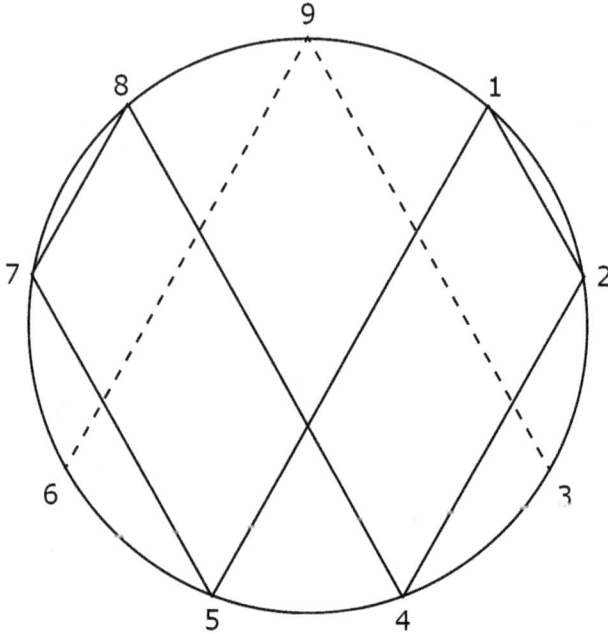

Figure 2-3: The Oscillating 3 & 6 with 9 as the Control

The number nine is unique in that it is the only number that represents the vertical axis. It never changes because it always equals itself. If you multiply 9 x 1 it equals nine, and 9 x 2 is eighteen, which is also equal to nine (1 + 8). You could take this out to infinity because the number 9 has no parity, but as you can tell from the above diagram, the other numbers do.

Number Parity

In Figure 2-4 below, you will see that I added a straight line going down from the nine through the bottom of the image between four and five. We see that the number nine represents the vertical axis going through the center of the image. Thus, if you were to fold the image in half along this axis, certain groups of numbers would coincide or lay on top of each other. These are the number pairs, "1" & "8", "2", & "7", "3" & "6", and "4" & "5". If you add the numbers that make up each of these pairs, they all equal the number nine.

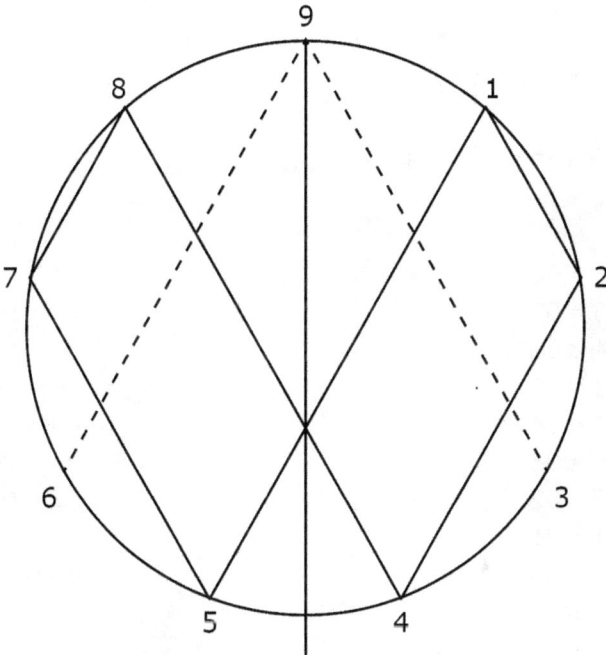

Figure 2-4: Number Parity

Another way to see the special relationship between these number pairs is through a simple multiplication series for each unique number one through eight. As stated earlier, all products are reduced to single digits through successive addition resulting in meaningful number sequences. In the following set, we see that each pair forms number sequences that are identical but in opposing directions going outwards from the center. In this manner, they can be said to "mirror" each other.

The 1 - 8 Pair

As you can see below, this depicts how the number "8" is the mirror of the number "1". In other words, they form a pair or have parity with each other.

91234567 **8** ⟵ Center ⟶ **1** 23456789

8 X 1 = 08 = 08	01 = 01 = 1 X 1
8 X 2 = 16 = 07	02 = 02 = 2 X 1
8 X 3 = 24 = 06	03 = 03 = 3 X 1
8 X 4 = 32 = 05	04 = 04 = 4 X 1
8 X 5 = 40 = 04	05 = 05 = 5 X 1
8 X 6 = 48 = 03	06 = 06 = 6 X 1
8 X 7 = 56 = 02	07 = 07 = 7 X 1
8 X 8 = 64 = 01	08 = 08 = 8 X 1
8 X 9 = 72 = 09	09 = 09 = 9 X 1

The 2 - 7 Pair

92468135 **7** ◄─── Center ───► **2** 46813579

7 X 1 = 07 = 07	02 = 02 = 1 X 2
7 X 2 = 14 = 05	04 = 04 = 2 X 2
7 X 3 = 21 = 03	06 = 06 = 3 X 2
7 X 4 = 28 = 01	08 = 08 = 4 X 2
7 X 5 = 35 = 08	01 = 10 = 5 X 2
7 X 6 = 42 = 06	03 = 12 = 6 X 2
7 X 7 = 49 = 04	05 = 14 = 7 X 2
7 X 8 = 56 = 02	07 = 16 = 8 X 2
7 X 9 = 63 = 09	09 = 18 = 9 X 2

The 3 - 6 Pair

93693693 **6** ◄─── Center ───► **3** 69369369

6 X 1 = 06 = 06	03 = 03 = 1 X 3
6 X 2 = 18 = 03	06 = 06 = 2 X 3
6 X 3 = 18 = 09	09 = 09 = 3 X 3
6 X 4 = 24 = 06	03 = 12 = 4 X 3
6 X 5 = 30 = 03	06 = 15 = 5 X 3
6 X 6 = 36 = 09	09 = 18 = 6 X 3
6 X 7 = 42 = 06	03 = 21 = 7 X 3
6 X 8 = 48 = 03	06 = 24 = 8 X 3
6 X 9 = 54 = 09	09 = 27 = 9 X 3

The 4 - 5 Pair

94837261 **5** ←— Center —→ **4** 83726159

5 X 1 = 05 = 05	04 = 04 = 1 X 4
5 X 2 = 10 = 01	08 = 08 = 2 X 4
5 X 3 = 15 = 06	03 = 12 = 3 X 4
5 X 4 = 20 = 02	07 = 16 = 4 X 4
5 X 5 = 25 = 07	02 = 20 = 5 X 4
5 X 6 = 30 = 03	06 = 24 = 6 X 4
5 X 7 = 35 = 08	01 = 28 = 7 X 4
5 X 8 = 40 = 04	05 = 32 = 8 X 4
5 X 9 = 45 = 09	09 = 36 = 9 X 4

Family Number Groups

Just like the parity that exists between certain sets of numbers as described above, there are also relationships that are based on thirds. In total there are three. One consists of the 1, 4, & 7, another consists of the 2, 5, & 8, and the other consists of the 3, 6, & 9. Looking back at Figure 2-4, notice that numbers within the first & second set occupy unique spatial characteristics with respect to the members of its family. For example, with respect to the vertical placement of numbers in the "1, 4, 7" family, the "1" occupies the very top position, "4" the very bottom, and "7" is in the middle. Likewise, with respect to the horizontal placement, the "1" & "4" occupy the right side, while the "7" occupies the left.

There is much more that could be said with respect to understanding numbers via Vortex-Based Mathematics, but for this work, the information thus far presented is sufficient. In the next chapter, I will be able to explain the connection between the diagram, the numerical relationships, and the order of planets in Vimshottari Dasha. If you would like to learn more about Vortex-Based Mathematics, I urge you to take a look at the work of Marko Rodin and Randy Powell.

3

THE STRUCTURE OF VEDIC ASTROLOGY

First and foremost, the fundamental structure of the Signs, Houses, and Nakshatras are based on a circle consisting of 360 degrees. There are a many theories and explanations in regards to why the ancients defined the circle as 360 degrees, but as it applies to vortex-based mathematics, it is a number of completion.

As I mentioned in the previous chapter, starting at the top of the circle at zero, and listing each number sequentially going around the circle, you get to the number nine when you return to the point of origin at zero. See Figure 3-1 on the following page. Whether it be eighteen "18", ninety "90", or one hundred seventy one "171", all of these numbers resolve to nine "9" and are thus indicative of completion or a return to the source. However, a unique quality of "360" that the others don't have is that it is also composed of digits that have a special relationship with nine per their family relationship based on thirds.

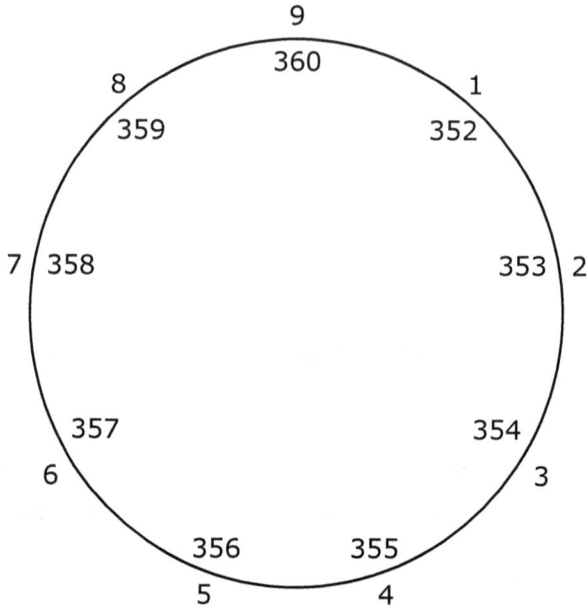

Figure 3: Nine as Number of Completion

The Signs

As for the origin of the Astrological Signs I refer the reader to a book entitled *Astrological Origins* by Cyril Fagan. In this book Fagan proposes the theory that the Signs originated in ancient Egypt and were key indicators of the agricultural year specific to that region. Among many of the things that Fagan brought to light, he proved that the ancient Egyptian day began at sunset similar to that of the Hebrews and many other ancient cultures. In similar fashion, the lunar month began at sunset when the thin disc of the crescent moon is viewable after the sun has set in the Western horizon. Full moons naturally occur in the opposite sign from the position of the sun 180 degrees away, which were important festival events to the ancient Egyptians.

One of the most important annual events in Egypt was the flooding of the Nile River in our modern day month of July. As an example, let's say that the Spring Equinox occurred when the sun was in 15 degrees of Aries. This means that at the Summer Solstice, the sun would be around 15 degrees of Cancer. When the annual flooding of the Nile began around July 15, the sun would set in Leo in the evening, but the stars rising in the East would be that of Aquarius. In Egypt, Aquarius is depicted as a man pouring out a jar of water. It perfectly matches the annual event of the Nile River flood. It was the stars rising in the East that governed the events of the year.

Cyril Fagan provided evidence that the 36 so-called Decans in the Zodiac of Denderah were in fact not Decans at all. The term Decan was a reference to the belief that each Decan represented 10 degrees of space, and that all 36 Decans represented the full circle of 360 degrees. Fagan showed that in fact they were Pentads representing 5 degrees of space. That on any particular night, the only visible constellations would consist of only half of the celestial sphere. Treating the so-called Decans as Pentads, the names given to these star clusters make more sense. One of these Pentads is Themat, which means the "river", and it tallies with the constellation of Aquarius.

In the next month, our modern day August, the sun would be in the constellation of Virgo, but at sunset, the stars rising in the East would be that of Pisces. Pisces is depicted as an image of two fish. Due to the increase of the Nile waters, we see why they would have derived such an image to match the events that were taking place on earth. On page 115 of *Astrological Origins* Fagan writes as follows,

> *"The oldest know so-called decan lists were found on coffin lids at Asyut, which Egyptologists assign to the IXth and Xth Heracleopolite dynasties, circa 2300 B.C. One of these decans shows a device of two fishes with the legend hnwy (khonuy). Treated as a pentade it synchronizes snugly with the constellation Pisces. Khonuy (Pisces) rose at sunset during August, when the Sun was in the opposite constellation, Virgo. At this time the inundation was so excessive as to turn almost the whole of Egypt into a sea, abounding in fish . . ."*

In the next month, our modern day September in which the Fall Equinox occurs, the sun would be in the constellation Libra, but at sunset, the stars rising in the East would be that of Aries, the Ram. On page 117 Fagan writes,

> *"This was the month of the autumnal equinox when the inundation was at its highest. Associated with Aries is Cetus, the Sea Monster. The waters of the nile were now so high that crocodiles and hippopotami swam over the erstwhile pastures. But in those pastures that remained dry, the ewes were separated from the rams at this period. In the decan lists and in the circular zodiac of Denderah, the ram is shown in a position of repose, indicative of sunset."*

In Egypt, the ram was a symbol for Amen. In the everyday speech "amen" means that which is hidden or concealed. Amen was used to describe the state of energy before creation took place as being at rest.

Going around the circle, constellation by constellation you can see a direct correspondence with Egyptian symbolism and the events of their year. For the last example, consider the month of March, which would have occurred when the sun was in Aries. As Cyril Fagan so aptly points out, no one is able to see the sun in any constellation because its light hides the stars from view. However, if you consider that at sunset, when the stars do become visible, the stars rising in the East are that of Libra.

In Egypt, Libra is depicted as a set of scales, which is one of the major symbols of the deity Maat. It indicates balance and equilibrium and a perfect picture to describe the occurrence of the Spring Equinox during the year. In the Zodiac of Dendera, also in the image of the scales is Heru-Pa-Khart rising out of a lotus flower within the disk of the sun over the symbol for the mount of sunrise. This only makes sense when you consider that the Spring Equinox is equivalent to sunrise in the daily cycle. It is the rebirth of the sun. Heru-Pa-Khart is Heru the child, who represents the young sun that was reborn.

Any time that we try to utilize the characteristics of a Sign based on its symbol, we are in error. We can't say that a person with Moon in Taurus is Bullish. It was a symbol during a certain time in Egypt indicating that after the flooding was over, the land was fertile and ready to be cultivated via plowing and the planting of new crops.

In Jyotish, the Signs are not used in error because the Signs are based on qualities that are distinct form the symbol itself. Each Sign possesses the qualities of one of the four elements. They are Fire, Earth, Air, and Water. Notice that in the structure of the Signs, this cycle repeats itself three times. It is very similar to the concept of thirds discussed in the previous chapter on Vortex-Based Mathematics. The first set of Signs – Aries through Cancer, is similar to the numbers one through three. The next set, Leo through Cancer is similar to the numbers four through six. The last set, Sagittarius through Pisces is similar to the numbers seven through nine.

Sign	Quality	Division
Aries	Fire	1st
Taurus	Earth	
Gemini	Air	
Cancer	Water	
Leo	Fire	2nd
Virgo	Earth	
Libra	Air	
Scorpio	Water	
Sagittarius	Fire	3rd
Capricorn	Earth	
Aquarius	Air	
Pisces	Water	

Navamsa

In Jyotish, another unique feature is the ninth part of a Sign called Navamsa. This was done to determine what Navamsa each of the planets were occupying in the natal chart. In essence, the Navamsa is able to provide a greater level of detail with respect to the Sign, but most important for this discussion is the fact that it is divided into nine parts. Each Sign being thirty degrees is divided by nine, making each Navamsa equal to three degrees twenty minutes of arc. Each Navamsa is labeled in the order of the Signs starting at zero degrees of Aries. In all, there are one hundred eight "108" divisions, which is another key number in the spiritual literature of many cultures. Notice that 1 + 0 + 8 is equal to nine "9", the number of completion.

Nakshatras

Another unique feature of Vedic Astrology is the use of Nakshatras or lunar mansions. There are a total of twenty seven "27" with each equaling 13 degrees 20 minutes of arc in a 360 degree circle. Once again, notice that twenty seven "27" can be reduced through successive addition to nine "9" (2 + 7). Just like the Signs, they are also based on thirds.

Each Nakshatra is assigned a planetary ruler in Jyotish. Since there are nine "9" unique planetary energies in the system, they repeat in sequence three times to complete the 27 divisions of space. They are assigned in the following order starting at 0 degrees of Aries. The same sequence will repeat itself at 0 degrees of Leo and 0 degrees of Sagittarius to complete the cycle.

Nakshatra Lord

Ketu
Venus
Sun
Moon
Mars
Rahu
Jupiter
Saturn
Mercury

In the previous chapter, we learned that in Vortex-Based Math, there are truly only nine "9" unique numbers in the universe as all numbers will resolve to one of the digits one to nine. Therefore, it is no surprise that in Jyotish, the sages defined nine "9" unique planetary energies in the system. The question is whether we can properly match the planetary energies with its numerical equivalent. As I discovered, this can indeed be accomplished.

4

THE ORDER OF PLANETS IN VIMSHOTTARI DASHA

In the first chapter, it was mentioned that upon seeing a connection between the structure of the Rig Veda and the order of planets in Vimshottari that Langenkamp believed the basis for the order of planets to be solid. This is because it is based on what he calls the primordial evolutionary sequence of nature as the Rig Veda is said to be an encyclopedia of all the laws of nature. I then suggested that in order to construct the Rig Veda - its first nine words, hymns, versus, and chapters, the author would most likely have possessed or had knowledge of a model with which to base the structure on. I then asked, what is this model? I believe it to be what Rodin calls Vortex-Based Mathematics.

"With . . . Vortex-Based Mathematics you will be able to see how energy is expressing itself mathematically. This math has no anomalies and shows the dimensional shape and function of the universe as being a toroid or donut-shaped black hole. This is the template for the universe . . ."[1]

As Rodin himself admits, this knowledge was well-known to the ancients, and is now being uncovered for us in this day & age.

In a previous chapter, Vortex-Based Mathematics showed us that there are only nine "9" unique numbers in the universe. Therefore, it is no surprise that in Jyotish, the sages recognized nine "9" unique planetary energies. Likewise, each of the nine "9" planets were assigned lordship over one of the nine periods in Vimshottari Dasha. After realizing the above, the question that came to my mind is whether the planetary lords have numerical equivalents in Vortex-Based Mathematics. As I will explain in the following pages of this chapter, they most certainly do.

In the introduction, the order of planets in Vimshottari Dasha was provided as per the following list below. It is composed of nine periods of varying lengths, each ruled by one of the nine planets of Vedic Astrology.

Dasha Ruler/Period	Length in Years
Ketu	7
Venus	20
Sun	6
Moon	10
Mars	7
Rahu	18
Jupiter	16
Saturn	19
Mercury	17

With the sequence of rulers set as above by the originator of Vimshottari Dasha, one realizes that there are only nine possible combinations of pairing the numbers one through nine with the planets. For example, one combination could pair Ketu with the number "1" with the remaining planets following in sequence so that Venus corresponds to the number "2", the Sun with number "3", and so on. This is depicted in the table below on the row labeled "Combo 1". The other combinations pair each of the eight remaining planets with the number "1" with planets following in sequence in the order of Vimshottari, but the main point is that after exhausting all possibilities you will only have nine sets of combinations or pairings. These are all listed in the table below.

	1	2	3	4	5	6	7	8	9
Combo 1	Ke	Ve	Su	Mo	Ma	Ra	Ju	Sa	Me
Combo 2	Ve	Su	Mo	Ma	Ra	Ju	Sa	Me	Ke
Combo 3	Su	Mo	Ma	Ra	Ju	Sa	Me	Ke	Ve
Combo 4	Mo	Ma	Ra	Ju	Sa	Me	Ke	Ve	Su
Combo 5	Ma	Ra	Ju	Sa	Me	Ke	Ve	Su	Mo
Combo 6	Ra	Ju	Sa	Me	Ke	Ve	Su	Mo	Ma
Combo 7	Ju	Sa	Me	Ke	Ve	Su	Mo	Ma	Ra
Combo 8	Sa	Me	Ke	Ve	Su	Mo	Ma	Ra	Ju
Combo 9	Me	Ke	Ve	Su	Mo	Ma	Ra	Ju	Sa

Now recall that certain sets of numbers mirror each other, or in other words they form pairs. If the planetary lords do have numerical equivalents in Vortex-Based Math, we should expect to find that the planets corresponding to the number pairs in one of the combinations from the table above should also mirror each other based on their said characteristics in Vedic Astrology. This is exactly what occurs if you pair Mercury with the number "1" as shown in Combo 9 above.

If you are familiar with the characteristics of the planets in Vedic Astrology you will notice right away that each of the now defined planetary pairs do in fact "mirror" each other. See Figure 4-1 below. Mercury corresponds to the number "1" and forms a pair with Jupiter who corresponds to the number "8". Ketu corresponds to the number "2" and forms a pair with Rahu who corresponds to the number "7". Venus corresponds to the number "3" and forms a pair with Mars who corresponds to the number "6". The Sun corresponds to number "4" and forms a pair with the Moon who corresponds to the number "5". Saturn corresponds to the number "9" and as stated in the previous chapter, this number has no parity.

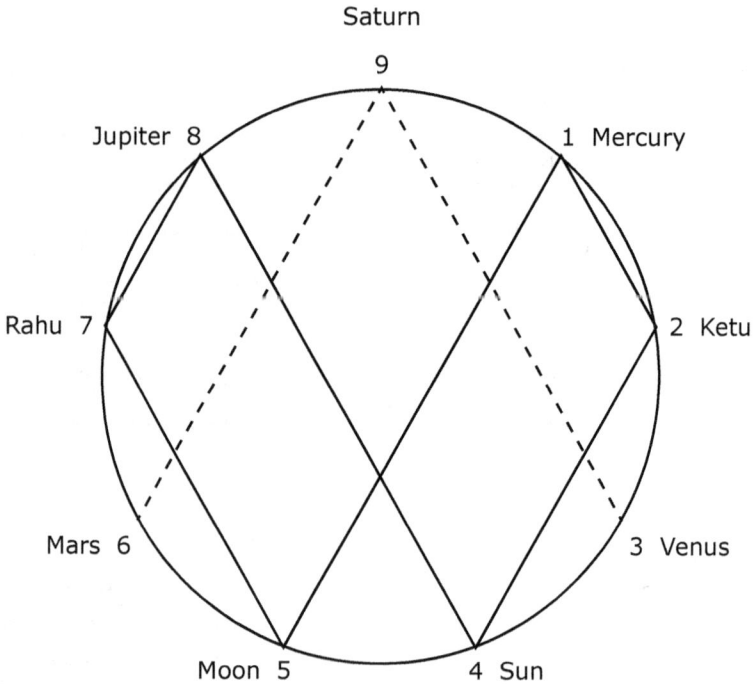

Figure 4-1: Planet to Number Relationships

What is noticeable right away is the fact that viewing the relationship of the planets in Vimshottari in this manner reveals the symmetry in how the planets are assigned rulership of the Rasis/Signs. Notice in the Zodiac depicted below that Mars rules the Rasis exactly opposite of Rasis that Venus rules. Likewise, Jupiter rules Rasis that are exactly opposite of the Rasis that Mercury rules. The Sun, the Moon, and Saturn also show symmetry in their rulerships. The Sun & Moon rule Rasis that are right next to each other as does Saturn, and these Rasis are exactly opposite of each other.

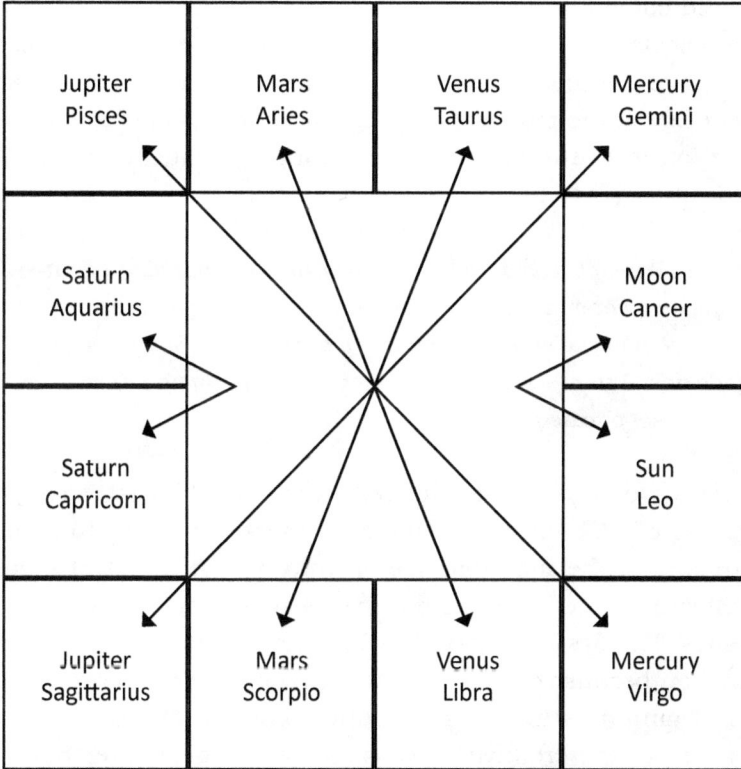

Jupiter Pisces	Mars Aries	Venus Taurus	Mercury Gemini
Saturn Aquarius			Moon Cancer
Saturn Capricorn			Sun Leo
Jupiter Sagittarius	Mars Scorpio	Venus Libra	Mercury Virgo

The opposing/mirroring nature of the planets as revealed in Figure 4-1 can also be seen throughout the spiritual literature and stories of many cultures. One with which I have personal experience and knowledge is that of ancient Kemet (Egypt). In ancient Kemet, the cosmological system was known as the Paut Neteru.

The Paut Neteru

A cosmogony can be defined as a model of the origin and evolution of the universe. It explains how the objects of the physical world come into manifestation. Since it traces the evolution of these objects from the beginning stage of creation, it also serves as a map of the underlying structure and order of the universe. In ancient Egypt, the model of the origin and evolution of the universe can be found in the material concerning the Paut Neteru or Tree of Life.

> *"The Tree of Life is a classification system composed of 11 categories wherein is classified all aspects of reality and their relationship to each other. Certain key attributes of God - so called deities, Neteru - serve as the theme or underlying principle of each set or category."*[2]

These categories are derived from the fact that creation is a process of differentiation where its most important function is the tracing of the maintenance of unity in the midst of increasing differentiation. Thus, within the creative process there are two extremes. The first is a state in which no things exist. There is no distinction because energy is at rest and matter is unformed. This is the beginning stage of the creative process. The second is the end result of the creative process where energy/matter has been modified into distinguishable forms. It is quite interesting that the things that take place between these two extremes are controlled by a set of nine "9" faculties, which are the Neteru or attributes of God as described in the quoted passage above.

There is no question that several versions of the Ennead or Company of the 9 Gods existed throughout the history of Kemet. However, there is one collection that I would like to use for the purpose of this chapter. It is the collection that Ra Un Nefer Amen presents in his book entitled *Metu Neter Vol. 2: Anuk Ausar: The Kamitic Initiation System*. Please refer to Figure 4-2 for a pictorial representation of the Tree of Life. Each of the numbered spheres 1 - 9 represents a particular Neteru who is responsible for a stage in the creative process. The sphere labeled zero "0" is the beginning stage where no things exist, and the sphere labeled ten "10" represents the end result of the creative process.

Amen

In the beginning stage of creation, even though there is no differentiation, the sages of Egypt still perceived the inherent duality of God & Woman's/Man's Being. They perceived that there is an intelligence or consciousness responsible for voluntary or willed behavior. Since consciousness/will cannot be divided, multiplied, added to or subtracted from, it is immaterial. This is our true identity - the Self. Consciousness is what we are and willing is what we do.

They also perceived a part of Being that is responsible for involuntary and automated behavior. It is composed of energy & matter which are polar opposites of each other. This aspect of Being is the Non-Self. Thus, the dual components of Being can be surmised in the following table.

COMPONENTS OF BEING			
Self/Identity/Immaterial		Not-Self/Non-Identity/Material	
Active	Passive	Active	Passive
Will	Consciousness	Energy	Mattter

In ancient Egypt, the word Amen means that which is hidden or concealed. It aptly describes the identity part of being because it is immaterial and hence cannot be divided, multiplied, etc. Therefore, it is imperceptible. Amen also aptly describes the Non-Identity part of being because at this stage of creation energy is at rest (peace) and matter is undifferentiated and yet to take on any form. Therefore, there are no things to perceive.

Ausar

Ausar corresponds to the sphere labeled one "1" on the Tree of Life. It is here that the components of Being described in the preceding stage are objectified. In the literature, we find that the Supreme Being Neb er Tcher (Lord of the World) is responsible for the work of creation in the form of Ausar. Thus, Ausar is indicative of the consciousness that is responsible for willed behavior. In one of the versions of the creation story we find Neb er Tcher saying,

> *"I was the creator of what came into being, that is to say, I formed myself out of the primeval matter, and I formed myself in the primeval matter. My name is Ausares [Ausar], who is the primeval matter of primeval matter."*[3]

The first matter is the formless matter as described in the preceding stage.

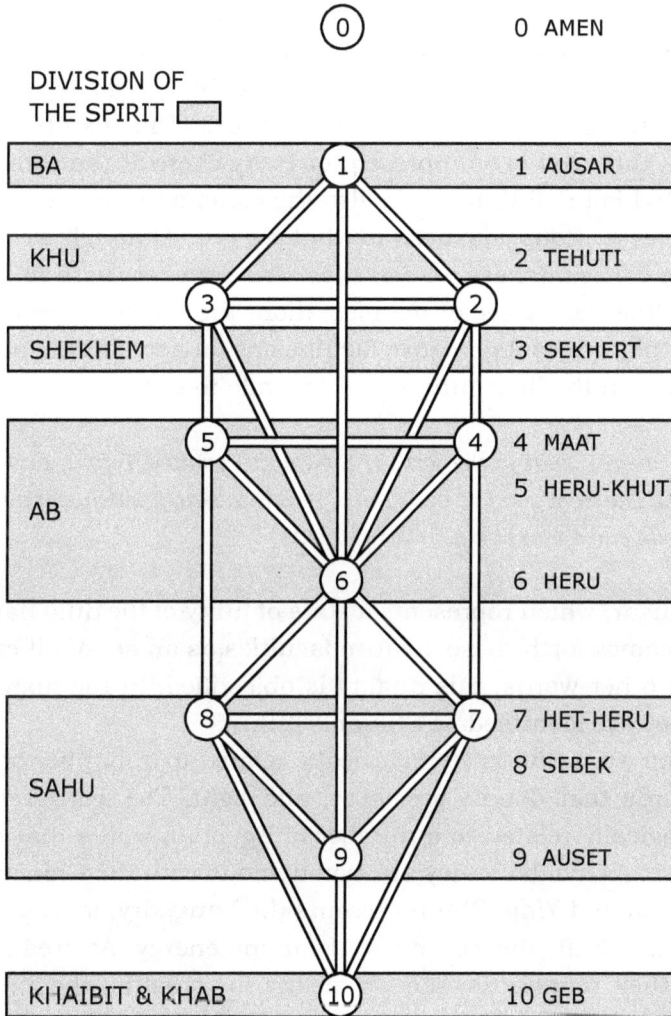

Figure 4-2: The Tree of Life

The metaphor corresponding to this sphere is unity. It accurately describes the fact that differentiation has yet to take place. Thus, the hieroglyphic representation of the name Ausar contains a picture of a single eye. It is telling us that Ausar is indicative of the consciousness that perceives or sees. This also brings out the idea that God is omnipresent or everywhere at the same time. Since God is in all things it is also the common source of unity in the universe. Consciousness is what we are. Although we cannot perceive consciousness we can experience oneness with it.

In the next stage of manifestation, the creator Ausar brings forth or objectifies its creative faculties as an act of differentiation. Therefore, in the literature, Ausar is made to say

> "I, even I, spat in the form of Shu, and I emitted Tefnut, and I became from god one gods three, that is to say, from myself two gods came into being on earth this."[4]

From Ausar, which represents a state of unity of the dual nature of Being, comes forth these creative faculties as an act of differentiation. In other words, this duality is objectified. In the above passage they are identified as Shu and Tefnut.

The word Shu is etymologically related to a number of Egyptian words that denote fire, heat, and light. The word Tefnut is etymologically related to a number of Egyptian words that denote moisture. As symbols they are synonymous with the Chinese concept of Yin and Ying. Shu represents the Yang, dry, masculine energy and Tefnut, the Yin, moist, feminine energy. As creative faculties, they represents Ausar's means for creating the universe. Therefore, Shu and Tefnut correspond to the 2nd and 3rd spheres of the Tree of Life, which corresponds to Tehuti and Sekhert, respectively.

Tehuti

Tehuti is the consciousness/will aspect of the dual nature of Being. The will is nothing more than the ability to choose or make a decision because it is a potential act. Therefore, this sphere corresponds to the will and potential acts of the creator. This is important to understand because the things that God wills are always in harmony with respect to the maintenance of unity, harmony, and order in the universe. This is why Tehuti is described as being the wisdom aspect of God's Being. It is thus why he is said to be omniscience or all-knowing.

As the 'God of Wisdom' in ancient Egypt, Tehuti is the patron of Oracles, which are devices used to consult the Will of God regarding a particular decision or action of the querent. Tehuti is also patron of sages who are nothing more than the men and women who have reached a level of spiritual development to become the living embodiment of the oracle. They are the mouthpiece of God from which issues forth wisdom or wise counsel. The counsel given by a sage or a high oracle that is designed to communicate with this aspect of God's being will always provide the best course of action with regards to a situation. If the action you carry out is in harmony with God's Will, it will create harmony and order in the universe.

Sekhert

Sekhert is indicative of the energy/matter aspect of the dual nature of Being. At this stage, energy is at rest and matter is formless and thus able to manifest all possibilities. Keep in mind that the consciousness/will aspect described in the preceding section is immaterial. It is the Self. Thus, the 3rd sphere represents the first objectification of the material part of being, which is Spirit. Energy & matter are nothing more than polarities of the material part of Being. To discuss the relationship between Tehuti as the immaterial part of Being and Sekhert as the material, I am going to use an analogy of the creative process between a man and woman in their efforts to create a child.

In order to create a child it takes the interaction of both male and female. A couple can come together at any time to conceive a child, and the male can deposit his seed at any time, but the female is only receptive to being impregnated at a specific time within her fertility cycle. Therefore, success is dependent on coming together at the proper time. The ability to conceive a child is subject to a time constraint dictated by the female fertility cycle which averages approximately 28 days and is marked by two key points. They are the times of ovulation and menstruation. The only time that a female can conceive is around the time of ovulation, which occurs around the midpoint between menstruations.

Using our analogy, we see that the Divine Will Tehuti corresponds to the male aspect, which has the potential to will or plant the seed at any time. Sekhert corresponds to the female aspect, which is the Divine Power that carries out the commands of the Will. Thus, in the Egyptian creation story it is said that Tehuti speaks (wills) the hekau (words of powers) residing in the 3rd sphere (Sekhert). The hekau are the eggs/molds or blueprint for everything in the universe. It is the action of speaking them that causes the inert energy to stir, vibrate, or cycle to begin the creative process. It is similar to our analogy because it is the female egg that is stirred to activity by the male seed, and begins to modify/ differentiate matter into the form of the child to be.

As the analogy informs us, Sekhert also corresponds to cycles, time constraints, and limitations. As some of you may have already deduced, these qualities ascribed to Sekhert sound a lot like the characteristics of the planet Saturn and you are right. In astrology Saturn is the planet that causes delays, which is analogous to the time constraint dictated by the female cycle as described above. In order to plant the seed at the right time to conceive, the cycle requires that you plan for the right moment when conditions are favorable. Interestingly, in Budge's hieroglyphic dictionary, the word 'skher (sekher)' means 'to plan'. The sages took this common everyday word and elevated it to the name of one of God's chief personifications to convey the fact that this power corresponds to the Divine Plan of the universe. It represents the underlying structure, blueprint, or design for everything in the universe. This is why the word 'skher' also means 'destiny'. Implicit in the concept of destiny is planning. If something is destined to occur in life it is because it was already planned to manifest.

Sekhert was depicted wrapped up in white cloth like that of Ausar. It shows that they are both in mummified form and therefore represent the inert powers of the night and death. Cyclically, Sekhert corresponds to the low point of any cycle. It is the point when energy returns to the source and becomes still and quite to regenerate before preparing for a new cycle of outward manifestation. This would correspond to the Winter Solstice in the yearly cycle and midnight in the daily. It is indicative of extreme cold like a body that has become cold, stiff, and rigid after death. It is a time when most of nature becomes still and at rest.

The tight wrapping of the cloth to which Sekhert and Ausar are bound also shows that they can't move and are hence inactive, stiff, and dead. It is telling of the state of energy at the 3rd sphere, which is inactive. Death is a metaphor for the ending of one cycle and the beginning of the next. It is thus that Sekhert corresponds to the tearing down of old structures in order to lay the foundation, structure, and plans for new ones.

Another Egyptian deity that corresponds to both Sekhert and Ausar is Ptah, who was also depicted in the tight fitting cloth indicating that he is in mummified form. Recall that it is through the interaction of Tehuti and Sekhert (Ausar's creative faculties) that he creates the world. In harmony with this concept, Ptah was said to carry into effect the commands issued by Tehuti concerning the creation of the universe. This is why we find the mergence of Ptah and Sekhert in the literature of Egypt. Budge writes that

> *"Ptah-Seker represents a personification of the union of the primeval creative power with a form of the inert powers of darkness, or in other words, Ptah-Seker is a form of Ausar, that is to say, of the night sun, or dead Sun-god."*[5]

Incidentally, it is not proper to think of Ra as the Sun-god, but it is instead similar to the concept of energy in physics or Chi in Chinese philosophy.

The first creative act produced by the interaction of Tehuti and Sekhert is to set energy/matter into motion.

> *"The first movement, the primeval impulse induced by the action of the will is spiral in form. Thus, the first act of creation was metaphorized . . . as the movement of a [two-headed] serpent, which was named Neheb Kau (the Provider of qualities or forms)."*[6]

In Egypt, one of the major symbols associated with Sekhert is the spiral. There were two hieroglyphs for the letter 'u'.

"One is the chick, and the other a spiral. It is interesting that many of the key words dealing with some aspect of creativity in which the u sound occurs, are written with the spiral. We find it in words such as "Ausares", the name of Ausar as creator; "Hekau", word of power; "Kheperu", creations; . . . "mesenu", to weave, to spin."[7]

It is noteworthy that the spiral bears a similar resemblance to the number nine. Figure 4-3 is an image of a spiral that I drew based on the Fibonacci number series 0, 1, 1, 2, 3, 5, 8, 13, etc. Notice how the spiral is similar in construction to the number nine.

In the number diagram as depicted in Figure 4-1 I showed how zero and nine occupy the same point on the circle. Zero is the starting point and going around the circle in sequence you complete a cycle when you get to the number nine at the beginning. It is the same with Sekhert who corresponds to the first objectification of energy/matter before differentiation begins. Sekhert represents the zero point of energy/matter. In addition, just as zero & nine represent the beginning and ending of the number cycle, so does Sekhert as described in the cycles of the day and year.

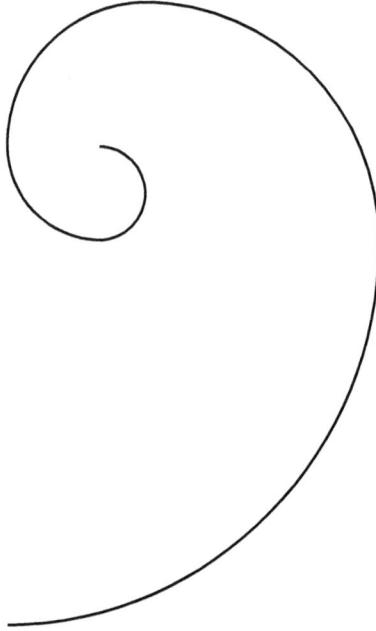

Figure 4-3: Fibonacci Spiral

In the Egyptian language, the "t" at the end of a word like the name Sekhert gives it a feminine connotation. Thus, in some instances you find that Sekhert takes on the feminine form and at others the masculine (Sekher). I find this interesting because if we refer back to our number diagram, we find that Saturn and the number nine have no parity with any other planet or number in the system. They stand alone on the central axis. Thus, we find that the Egyptian custom of using Sekhert in both the feminine and masculine form is in harmony with this correspondence to the number nine.

Jupiter & Mercury

These two planets rule Rasis/Signs that are opposite each other in the Zodiac. Mercury rules Gemini & Virgo while Jupiter rules Sagittarius & Pisces. Mithuna/Gemini is opposite the sign of Dhanus/Sagittarius and Kanya/Virgo is opposite the sign of Meena/Pisces. In addition to the above, these two planets mirror each other in their characteristics.

Venus & Mars

Venus rules Taurus and Libra while Mars rules Scorpio and Aries. These two planets also rule Rasis/Signs that are opposite each other in the Zodiac. Just like Jupiter & Mercury, their characteristics are opposite of each other. Venus is peace loving and sociable, preferring an environment where everybody gets along. Mars on the other hand has a combative and competitive nature.

The Sun & Moon

The same can be said of the Sun & Moon. The are the opposite of each other in their characteristics. The Sun represents the father while the Moon represents the mother.

Rahu & Ketu

Ketu is the south node of the moon and Rahu is the north node. They are opposing points of the Moon's orbit where it crosses the ecliptic. In the literature they each have characteristics that are the opposite of each other.

With the number to planetary relationships set as in the image below, it must be noted that there is a very small percentage of ways in which the planets of Vimshottari Dasha could have been ordered so that its pairs match the number sequence pairs in this manner. That is, that they are ordered in a way so that certain planetary pairs correspond to the number pairs. In fact, with nine planets in the system, they could have been arranged in a total of 362,880 different ways. However, the originator of Vimshottari chose one that corresponds neatly to the number pairs shown below when Saturn is made to correspond with the number nine "9".

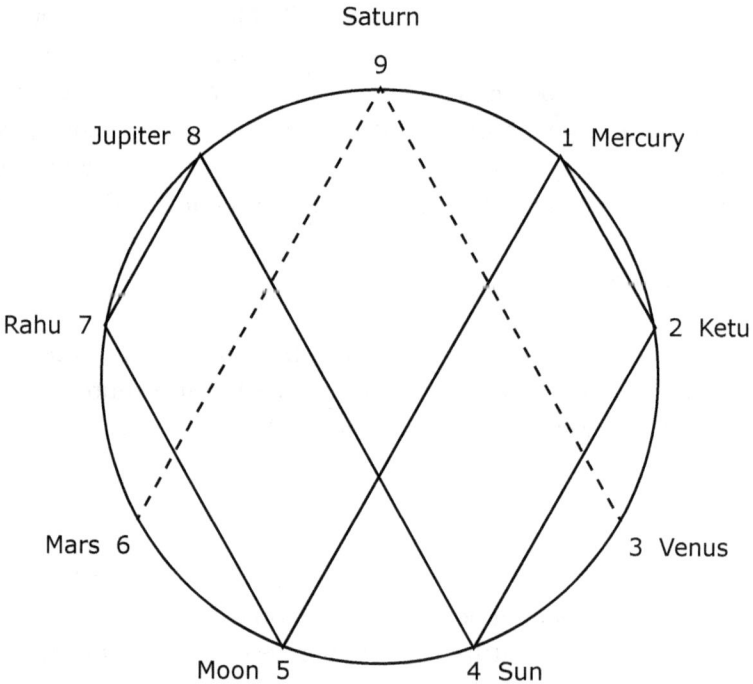

It is my belief that the originator of this system was well aware of the number patterns and relationships as explained via Vortex-Based Mathematics. Maybe the planets of Vimshottari Dasha were arranged to reflect this hidden numerology - an understanding of the special relationship between certain numbers and their mechanical properties. I find it quite amazing that they can be listed in sequence around a circle and form very recognizable pairs based on the qualities and characteristics. I don't believe this to be just a coincidence. With 362,880 possible ways to arrange these nine planets, the odds that it was just chance is very low.

ENDNOTES

CHAPTER 4

[1] Rodin, Marko. (n.d.). "Introduction of Rodin Coil and Votex Based Mathematics." Retrieved 20 December 2009. http://www.markorodin.com/content/view/7/26/

[2] Amen, Ra Un Nefer, *Metu Neter Vol. 2: Anuk Ausar: The Kamitic Initiation System*, p. 59.

[3] Budge, E. A. Wallis, *The Gods of the Egyptians Vol. 1: Studies in Egyptian Mythology*, P. 300.

[4] Ibid, p. 317

[5] Ibid, p. 503

[6] Amen, Ra Un Nefer, *Metu Neter Vol. 2: Anuk Ausar: The Kamitic Initiation System*, p. 45.

[7] Ibid, p. 47

~

BIBLIOGRAPHY

Amen, Ra Un Nefer, *Metu Neter Vol. 2: Anuk Ausar: The Kamitic Initiation System*, Brooklyn: Khamit Corp., 1994. Print.

Braha, James T., *Ancient Hindu Astrology For The Modern Western Astrologer*, Hollywood: Hermetician Press, 1986. Print.

Budge, E. A. Wallis, *The Gods of the Egyptians Vol. 1: Studies in Egyptian Mythology*, Dover Publications, Inc., Mineola, NY, 1969

Fagan, Cyril, *Astrological Origins*, St. Paul: Llewellyn Publications, 1971. Print.

Houck, Richard, *Hindu Astrology Lessons: 36 Teachers Share Their Wisdom*, Gaithersburg: Groundswell Press, 1997. Print.

Kar, K.R., "In Quest of Origin of Parasar's Vimshottary Dasa - Period." *K.P. Year Book,* 2004.

Langenkamp, Frans, "The Basis of the Vimshottary Dasha System found in Rig Veda." *Saptarishis Astrology Online Magazine, Volume VIII* - June 2010.

Naik, Satyanarayana, *K.P. Dynamics: Stellar Horary Astrology Redefined,* Hyderabad: Sri Jayalakshmi Publications, 2007. Print.

Parasara, *Brihat Parasara Hora Sastra,* Ed. Trans. R. Santhanam. New Delhi: Ranjan Publications, 2009. Print.

Rele, V. G., *Directional Astrology of the Hindus as Propounded in Vimshattari Dasa,* Bombay: D. B. Taraporevala Sons & Co., 1935. Print.

Rodin, Marko. (n.d.), "Introduction of Rodin Coil and Votex Based Mathematics." Retrieved 20 December 2009. http://www. markorodin.com/content/view/7/26/

ALSO AVAILALE FROM THE AUTHOR

W.D. GANN: DIVINATION BY MATHEMATICS

W.D. GANN: DIVINATION BY MATHEMATICS: HARMONIC
ANALYSIS

OBSERVATIONS ON W.D. GANN VOL. 1: PERIODICITY